Francis Frith's
Worcester

Photographic Memories

Francis Frith's
Worcester

Julie Meech

FRITH
BOOK Co

First published in the United Kingdom in 2001 by
Frith Book Company Ltd

Hardback Edition 2001
ISBN 1-85937-395-x

Paperback Edition 2001
ISBN 1-85937-165-5

British Library Cataloguing in Publication Data

Francis Frith's Worcester
Julie Meech

Frith Book Company Ltd
Frith's Barn, Teffont,
Salisbury, Wiltshire SP3 5QP
Tel: +44 (0) 1722 716 376
Email: info@francisfrith.co.uk
www.francisfrith.co.uk

Printed and bound in Great Britain

Front Cover: Worcester, Broad Street 1955 w141022

AS WITH ANY HISTORICAL DATABASE THE FRITH ARCHIVE IS CONSTANTLY BEING CORRECTED AND IMPROVED
AND THE PUBLISHERS WOULD WELCOME INFORMATION ON OMISSIONS OR INACCURACIES

Contents

Francis Frith: *Victorian Pioneer*

FRANCIS FRITH, Victorian founder of the world-famous photographic archive, was a complex and multi-talented man. A devout Quaker and a highly successful Victorian businessman, he was both philosophic by nature and pioneering in outlook.

By 1855 Francis Frith had already established a wholesale grocery business in Liverpool, and sold it for the astonishing sum of £200,000, which is the equivalent today of over £15,000,000. Now a multi-millionaire, he was able to indulge his passion for travel. As a child he had pored over travel books written by early explorers, and his fancy and imagination had been stirred by family holidays to the sublime mountain regions of Wales and Scotland. 'What a land of spirit-stirring and enriching scenes and places!' he had written. He was to return to these scenes of grandeur in later years to 'recapture the thousands of vivid and tender memories', but with a different purpose. Now in his thirties, and captivated by the new science of photography, Frith set out on a series of pioneering journeys to the Nile regions that occupied him from 1856 until 1860.

Intrigue and Adventure

He took with him on his travels a specially-designed wicker carriage that acted as both dark-room and sleeping chamber. These far-flung journeys were packed with intrigue and adventure. In his life story, written when he was sixty-three, Frith tells of being held captive by bandits, and of fighting 'an awful midnight battle to the very point of surrender with a deadly pack of hungry, wild dogs'. Sporting flowing Arab costume, Frith arrived at Akaba by camel seventy years before Lawrence, where he encountered 'desert princes and rival sheikhs, blazing with jewel-hilted swords'.

During these extraordinary adventures he was assiduously exploring the desert regions bordering the Nile and patiently recording the antiquities and peoples with his camera. He was the first photographer to venture beyond the sixth cataract. Africa was still the mysterious 'Dark Continent', and Stanley and Livingstone's historic meeting was a decade into the future. The conditions for picture taking confound belief. He laboured for hours in his wicker dark-room in the sweltering heat of the desert, while the volatile chemicals fizzed dangerously in their trays. Often he was forced to work in remote tombs and caves where conditions were cooler. Back in London he exhibited his photographs and was 'rapturously cheered' by members of the Royal Society. His reputation as a

photographer was made overnight. An eminent modern historian has likened their impact on the population of the time to that on our own generation of the first photographs taken on the surface of the moon.

Venture of a Life-Time

Characteristically, Frith quickly spotted the opportunity to create a new business as a specialist publisher of photographs. He lived in an era of immense and sometimes violent change. For the poor in the early part of Victoria's reign work was a drudge and the hours long, and people had precious little free time to enjoy themselves. Most had no transport other than a cart or gig at their disposal, and had not travelled far beyond the boundaries of their own town or village. However,

by the 1870s, the railways had threaded their way across the country, and Bank Holidays and half-day Saturdays had been made obligatory by Act of Parliament. All of a sudden the ordinary working man and his family were able to enjoy days out and see a little more of the world.

With characteristic business acumen, Francis Frith foresaw that these new tourists would enjoy having souvenirs to commemorate their days out. In 1860 he married Mary Ann Rosling and set out with the intention of photographing every city, town and village in Britain. For the next thirty years he travelled the country by train and by pony and trap, producing fine photographs of seaside resorts and beauty spots that were keenly bought by millions of Victorians. These prints were painstakingly pasted into family albums and pored over during the dark nights of winter, rekindling precious memories of summer excursions.

The Rise of Frith & Co

Frith's studio was soon supplying retail shops all over the country. To meet the demand he gathered about him a small team of photographers, and published the work of independent artist-photographers of the calibre of Roger Fenton and Francis Bedford. In order to gain some understanding of the scale of Frith's business one only has to look at the catalogue issued by Frith & Co in 1886: it runs to some 670 pages, listing not only many thousands of views of the British Isles but also many photographs of most European countries, and China, Japan, the USA and Canada – note the sample page shown above from the hand-written *Frith & Co* ledgers detailing pictures taken. By 1890 Frith had created the greatest specialist photographic publishing company in the world,

Frith's death, a new card measuring 5.5 x 3.5 inches became the standard format, but it was not until 1902 that the divided back came into being, with address and message on one face and a full-size illustration on the other. *Frith & Co* were in the vanguard of postcard development, and Frith's sons Eustace and Cyril continued their father's monumental task, expanding the number of views offered to the public and recording more and more places in Britain, as the coasts and countryside were opened up to mass travel.

Francis Frith died in 1898 at his villa in Cannes, his great project still growing. The archive he created continued in business for another seventy years. By 1970 it contained over a third of a million pictures of 7,000 cities, towns and villages. The massive photographic record Frith has left to us stands as a living monument to a special and very remarkable man.

with over 2,000 outlets – more than the combined number that Boots and W H Smith have today! The picture on the right shows the *Frith & Co* display board at Ingleton in the Yorkshire Dales. Beautifully constructed with mahogany frame and gilt inserts, it could display up to a dozen local scenes.

Postcard Bonanza

The ever-popular holiday postcard we know today took many years to develop. In 1870 the Post Office issued the first plain cards, with a pre-printed stamp on one face. In 1894 they allowed other publishers' cards to be sent through the mail with an attached adhesive halfpenny stamp. Demand grew rapidly, and in 1895 a new size of postcard was permitted called the court card, but there was little room for illustration. In 1899, a year after

Frith's Archive: *A Unique Legacy*

FRANCIS FRITH'S legacy to us today is of immense significance and value, for the magnificent archive of evocative photographs he created provides a unique record of change in 7,000 cities, towns and villages throughout Britain over a century and more. Frith and his fellow studio photographers revisited locations many times down the years to update their views, compiling for us an enthralling and colourful pageant of British life and character.

We tend to think of Frith's sepia views of Britain as nostalgic, for most of us use them to conjure up memories of places in our own lives with which we have family associations. It often makes us forget that to Francis Frith they were records of daily life as it was actually being lived in the cities, towns and villages of his day. The Victorian age was one of great and often bewildering change for ordinary people, and though the pictures evoke an impression of slower times, life was as busy and hectic as it is today.

We are fortunate that Frith was a photographer of the people, dedicated to recording the minutiae of everyday life. For it is this sheer wealth of visual data, the painstaking chronicle of changes in dress, transport, street layouts, buildings, housing, engineering and landscape that captivates us so much today. His remarkable images offer us a powerful link with the past and with the lives of our ancestors.

Today's Technology

Computers have now made it possible for Frith's many thousands of images to be accessed almost instantly. In the Frith archive today, each photograph is carefully 'digitised' then stored on a CD Rom. Frith archivists can locate a single photograph amongst thousands within seconds. Views can be catalogued and sorted under a variety of categories of place and content to the immediate benefit of researchers.

Inexpensive reference prints can be created for them at the touch of a mouse button, and a wide range of books and other printed materials assembled and published for a wider, more general readership - in the next twelve months over a hundred Frith local history titles will be published! The day-to-day workings of the archive are very different from how they were in Francis Frith's time: imagine the herculean task of sorting through eleven tons of glass negatives as Frith had to do to locate a particular sequence of pictures! Yet

See Frith at www. frithbook.co.uk

the archive still prides itself on maintaining the same high standards of excellence laid down by Francis Frith, including the painstaking cataloguing and indexing of every view.

It is curious to reflect on how the internet now allows researchers in America and elsewhere greater instant access to the archive than Frith himself ever enjoyed. Many thousands of individual views can be called up on screen within seconds on one of the Frith internet sites, enabling people living continents away to revisit the streets of their ancestral home town, or view places in Britain where they have enjoyed holidays. Many overseas researchers welcome the chance to view special theme selections, such as transport, sports, costume and ancient monuments.

We are certain that Francis Frith would have heartily approved of these modern developments in imaging techniques, for he himself was always working at the very limits of Victorian photographic technology.

The Value of the Archive Today

Because of the benefits brought by the computer, Frith's images are increasingly studied by social historians, by researchers into genealogy and ancestory, by architects, town planners, and by teachers and schoolchildren involved in local history projects.

In addition, the archive offers every one of us an opportunity to examine the places where we and our families have lived and worked down the years. Highly successful in Frith's own era, the archive is now, a century and more on, entering a new phase of popularity.

The Past in Tune with the Future

Historians consider the Francis Frith Collection to be of prime national importance. It is the only archive of its kind remaining in private ownership and has been valued at a million pounds. However, this figure is now rapidly increasing as digital technology enables more and more people around the world to enjoy its benefits.

Francis Frith's archive is now housed in an historic timber barn in the beautiful village of Teffont in Wiltshire. Its founder would not recognize the archive office as it is today. In place of the many thousands of dusty boxes containing glass plate negatives and an all-pervading odour of photographic chemicals, there are now ranks of computer screens. He would be amazed to watch his images travelling round the world at unimaginable speeds through network and internet lines.

The archive's future is both bright and exciting. Francis Frith, with his unshakeable belief in making photographs available to the greatest number of people, would undoubtedly approve of what is being done today with his lifetime's work. His photographs, depicting our shared past, are now bringing pleasure and enlightenment to millions around the world a century and more after his death.

Worcester - *An Introduction*

FOR OVER 2,000 years there has been a settlement at Worcester, as numerous Iron Age finds indicate. It owes its origin to the River Severn, which was fordable at this point at low tide, making it the only crossing point between Gloucester and Bridgnorth, and therefore of both practical and strategic importance. A small farming community developed initially, and only attained a degree of prominence in the Roman period, after the 20th Legion built a road along the east bank of the Severn, linking forts at Kingsholm (Gloucester) and Wroxeter (near Shrewsbury). What was later to become Worcester lay on the route of the road and soon developed into a river port, (possibly called Vertis) mainly for transporting salt brought from the mines at Droitwich.

Despite the beginnings of trade and commerce, Worcester's economy was still mainly agrarian, exploiting the fertile soils of the river terraces. However, in the 2nd century a major iron smelting industry developed, which seems to have begun in the Deansway/Broad Street area of the city, close to the river. Despite the importance of the iron smelting operations, Worcester was never in the first rank of Roman towns. It does, however, seem to have become a flourishing industrial and commercial centre which made good use of its rich agricultural hinterland. This probably ensured its survival in the years of instability which began in the late 3rd century. Worcester's growth was reversed and iron production ceased, but unlike many other settlements, it did survive continuing instability,

Roman withdrawal in the 5th century and the remorseless spread of invading Angles, Saxons and Jutes across the country.

After the Romans left, a British community seems to have established control over Worcester until the 7th century, when it became part of the Anglo-Saxon kingdom of the Hwicce, whose power base was at Winchcombe in Gloucestershire. In c680 Worcester acquired a cathedral dedicated to St Peter, and a bishop called Bosel. Weogornaceaster, as the Anglo-Saxons called the town, became an increasingly important religious centre, with the wealth of the church acting as a stimulus for commerce.

In the 890s Aethelred of Mercia refortified Worcester, which acquired earth walls and ditches, establishing it as a 'burh' (fortified borough) and administrative centre, and marking a significant step forward. It established the structure around which the later medieval town was to develop - a structure still visible in today's street plan. Bishop (later Saint) Oswald founded a monastic community of Benedictines for whom he built a new cathedral (next to St Peter's) dedicated to Christ and St Mary. Completed by 983, the site of Oswald's cathedral lies beneath the present building. Late Saxon Worcester had become a prosperous town, ecclesiastically important and with a valuable agricultural hinterland. Its economy was based on trade and local manufacturing,

supplemented by taxes levied on river and road traffic passing through. Nevertheless, Viking raids into the Severn Valley must have added a touch of uncertainty to daily life, and on one memorable occasion in 1041, the Danish King Harthacnut tried to raise taxes from Worcester. The king's would-be tax collector was murdered by outraged citizens and his flayed skin nailed to the cathedral door (where traces of it remained for centuries). Harthacnut sent a retaliatory raiding party, but the citizens took refuge on Bevere Island upriver and the Danes contented themselves with sacking the town and burning the cathedral before they left the area.

When the Normans arrived they found a well-established town, with the foundations already laid for the important medieval city which was to develop. Under the leadership of Urse d'Abitot, Sheriff of Worcester from 1069, the Normans built a castle, of which no trace remains. Wulfstan, the Saxon bishop, was allowed to stay in office and rebuilt the cathedral between 1084 and 1089 on the site of St Mary's. Some fragments of his building still survive, notably the crypt. Respected by Saxons and Normans alike, Bishop (later Saint) Wulfstan had considerable influence and helped Worcester become the most important ecclesiastical centre in the West Midlands.

The 12th and 13th centuries were turbulent times for Worcester due to the endless squabbling between kings and nobles. The strategic nature of

the river crossing meant everybody was keen to control it. The Civil War (1135-54) of King Stephen's reign was a particularly bad time, especially when the king captured and burnt the city, but it was only one of numerous conflicts throughout these two centuries. It is not surprising that substantial city walls were deemed necessary, and they were completed some time during King John's reign. Nevertheless, Worcester prospered: by the 14th century it had a cathedral, 11 churches and four monastic communities. Its suburbs were spreading north along Foregate Street and The Tything, east along Lowesmoor and south along Sidbury, while the suburb of St John's was taking shape across the river. In 1377 the population was 3,000; by the 16th century it had grown to 8,000. The community engaged in an enormous variety of trades and crafts and traded with France, Germany, Spain, Iceland and the Low Countries. Cloth and clothing manufacture came to dominate the economy in the 15th century and the city acquired an international reputation for its products.

During the 16th and 17th centuries it began to look as though the good times were over. Other Severn Valley towns were eroding Worcester's regional dominance and the clothing industry was in decline. In 1637 the city was badly hit by plague, which killed perhaps one in ten of the population. Then came the Civil War: Worcester, strategically important as ever, found itself once more in the thick of the action. Both the first skirmish (1642) and the final battle (1651) were fought in or close to the city, and after Charles I's victory at Edgehill, Worcester became a Royalist garrison. In 1646 it withstood three months of siege before surrendering. During the siege some medieval suburbs were deliberately destroyed by the garrison to prevent the Parliamentarians approaching too close to the city walls. Further massive damage took place during the Battle of Worcester in 1651 and it is not surprising that the city has few surviving medieval buildings. Ordinary citizens must have been deeply resentful of both sides in the Civil War, but what was perceived as Worcester's staunch loyalty to the Stuart cause earned it the name Faithful City.

Despite the disruption and destruction, Worcester got back to business as soon as the fighting stopped. A 1661 census listed it as the 11th city of the kingdom and it flourished anew in the late 17th century, making good use of its position by the Severn. Indeed, it is hard to overstate the importance of the river in the city's history. Though its strategic significance often brought conflict, its principal role for most of its history has been a commercial one. By the end of the 17th century the Severn was busier than any other European river, except the Meuse, and Worcester was one of its principal ports.

Superficially at least, Worcester prospered

throughout the 18th and 19th centuries, but this was deceptive. The city needed to diversify its manufacturing base and to improve its infrastructure, but it did neither. Too much of the population was still dependent on the declining clothing industry (particularly glove making) with its desperately low wages. All the money lavished by the wealthy on grand houses and churches could not altogether hide the fact that a huge underclass lived in great poverty in squalid slums. Some efforts were made to address the problem, particularly by local Whigs, and it was partly to reduce unemployment that in 1751 a group of businessmen founded the Worcester Porcelain Works. By 1788 a rival firm, Chamberlain & Co, had set up on Severn Street. In that same year George III, in town to enjoy the Three Choirs Festival, toured the Severn Street works and ordered three dinner services for the royal household. The company received the royal warrant in 1789 and the internationally renowned Royal Worcester, formed from a merger of the rivals, still operates from the same site today.

Severn trade was given a welcome boost by the growing canal system: the Droitwich Canal, the Staffordshire and Worcestershire, and the Worcester and Birmingham all played their part, but major improvements were needed on the river itself. Though the Severn was tidal up to Worcester, and navigable almost as far as Welshpool, the navigation

had never been an easy one. Water levels were very low in summer and above Gloucester the river was little more than a series of pools separated by rock bars with minimal depth of water above them. In 1827 the completion of the Gloucester and Sharpness Canal boosted trade by enabling traffic on the lower Severn to bypass the river, but the opening of the Birmingham and Gloucester Railway in 1841 led to a reduction in canal traffic. It was only between 1842 and 1844 that the navigation of the upper Severn was at last improved. Locks and weirs were built, causing the upper tidal limit to move south to Gloucester, and the river was dredged. In 1890 further improvements were made to encourage larger vessels from the channel ports, but the river and canals were losing out heavily to the railway, even though Worcester's rail links were, and remain, inadequate. The 20th-century growth of road transport dealt the final blow, though it was 1961 before the last commercial cargo left Diglis Basin by narrowboat.

In 1826 the government abolished import duty on foreign gloves, a move which brought about the end of Worcester's gloving industry. Other industries sprang up, such as brewing, bottle making, vinegar production and engineering. Throughout the late 19th century conditions for the urban poor slowly began to improve, with increased provision of fresh water and better sanitation, though it was only in the 1920s that slum clearance

began. Housing for the better off, however, expanded considerably through the late Victorian and Edwardian periods. Later, in the 1960s, massive redevelopment of the city centre involved the wholesale demolition of most of the remaining ancient buildings, and the imposition of a brutal road system, cutting the cathedral off from High Street. It made Worcester a byword for how not to do things.

After the M5 replaced the Severn and the canals as a trading route, Worcester became important for distribution and light engineering and over the last two decades it has expanded again. In the centre, an effort has been made to make further redevelopment more sympathetic to the historic fabric and some (though not nearly enough) of the 60s horrors have been swept away. Nothing can restore what has been lost; yet it is not all bad news. The medieval street pattern remains clearly visible, as do stretches of the city walls. The cathedral and the monastic ruins, together with Edgar Tower and the 15th-, 16th- and 17th-century buildings of Friar Street, New Street and Corn Market hint at the glory

that was medieval Worcester. There is an abundance of elegant Georgian architecture and some good Victorian buildings too, of both the exuberant, flamboyant type and the solid, sensible variety. Despite all that has been lost, Worcester is still a rewarding city to explore and tourism is today playing an increasingly important part in its economy.

An added attraction is that every third year the city hosts Europe's oldest musical festival, the Three Choirs, which it has shared with Hereford and Gloucester since 1719. The music of Worcester's most famous son, Sir Edward Elgar, often features in the festival programme. Other tastes in music and the arts are well catered for, and sport is important too, with the bonus that the county cricket ground is generally agreed to be the most attractive in the country. The River Severn continues to play an important role, pleasure steamers sharing the water with canoes, dragon boats, cruisers and an abundance of narrowboats whose owners (or hirers) are now bent on pleasure, not commerce.

Worcester

Worcester
The Cathedral and Bridge 1891 29296
The majestic cathedral overlooks the bridge designed by John Gwynn in
1781, replacing a medieval structure built c1313, which was upstream
from the present site. Gwynn's bridge had already been widened by 1847,
long before this photograph was taken, but no major reconstruction took
place until the 1930s. The laden barge in the foreground is a reminder of
the days when the River Severn was the busiest trade route in Britain. At
one time, North Quay (on the left) would have been crowded with boats,
but by 1891 the railways had taken over, leaving Severn trade to stagnate.

▼ **Worcester, The Cathedral from the River Severn 1891** 29301
This tranquil view, taken from the west bank of the Severn, includes
not only the cathedral but also All Saints' Church and St Andrew's.
The photographer is standing on the edge of Chapter Meadows,
which are still cut for hay every July, then grazed by cattle through
late summer and autumn, as they have been since Roman times.

▼ **Worcester, The Cathedral 1923** 73749
Though the cathedral was begun in 1084, the exterior is largely the
result of 13th- and 14th-century rebuilding and 19th-century
restoration. The original tower, for instance, collapsed in 1175 and its
replacement was not completed until 1374. It stands nearly 200 ft high
and, apparently, weighs 4,100 tons - but how do they know that?

▲ **Worcester
The Cathedral, West
Front 1891** 29298
This classic view shows
to good advantage the
central tower and the
west window. Designed
c1870 by Sir George
Gilbert Scott, with glass
by Hardman's of
Birmingham, the window
depicts the biblical story
of the Creation. A rather
similar view of the
cathedral and the
Jacobean house to its left
appears on the current
£20 bank note.

◀ **Worcester, The Monastic Ruins 1891** 29307
This is all that remains of the Guesten House, built in 1320 for visitors to the monastery. By 1862 it was dilapidated and to save the expense of restoration and upkeep it was demolished, except for one wall, deliberately left as a 'picturesque' ruin. The roof was saved and can now be seen at Avoncroft Museum of Buildings, near Bromsgrove.

◄ **Worcester, South Quay
1910** 62329
A party composed
mostly of ladies in long
flowing skirts enjoys a
pleasant stroll between
the river and the
monastic ruins which
adjoin the cathedral. The
riverside promenade is
said to be built on a
foundation of rubble-
filled barges sunk in the
19th century. Today, this
bleak scene is much
more leafy, thanks to
extensive tree planting.

Worcester
The Cathedral and
Monastic Ruins 1892
29884
These ruins stand between the cathedral and the River Severn and are those of the monks' reredorter, or lavatories, conveniently sited to enable the drains to discharge straight into the river.

Worcester
The Cathedral
The Crypt 1893 32101
The earliest surviving structure in Worcester, and the largest Norman crypt in England, this is all that remains of St Wulfstan's cathedral of 1084. Built partly of reused masonry from St Oswald's Benedictine Priory, it is very beautiful, with a forest of stone columns supporting a simple vaulted roof.

Worcester, The Cathedral Quire
1891 29313
The photographer was standing below the high altar to take this view, which looks westwards the length of the quire and nave to the great west window. The tomb in the foreground is that of King John (1167-1216), the first post-Conquest monarch to be buried in England. He lies here at Worcester at his own request. In 1218 the remains of Worcester's two great saints, Wulfstan and Oswald, were transferred from their original tombs to a shrine in the quire and John was buried between them - they are represented by two small figures either side of his shoulders.

Worcester, The Cathedral, Rising from the Dead 1907 59094
The Dean's chapel in the south quire transept has a 13th-century frieze of carvings in the spandrels of the arcading (that is, between the tops of the adjoining arches). Those on the south wall feature scenes from Judgement Day, including these three members of the faithful pushing up their coffin lids as they rise from the dead.

Worcester, The Cathedral, The Pulpit 1893 32095
Red marble lions (one just visible here) guard the steps which rise to the ornate pulpit, carved from red, green and cream marble. Designed by Sir George Gilbert Scott and made by William Forsyth, this is Victorian art at its most florid. It stands in the nave: there is a restrained and elegant 17th-century pulpit in the chancel.

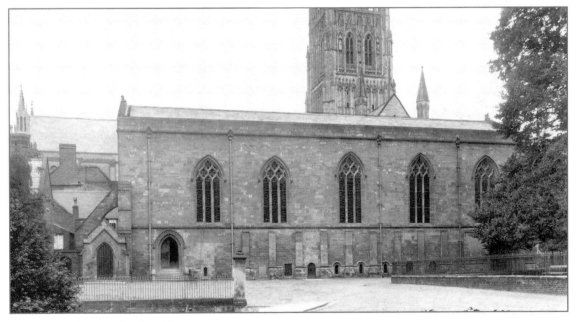

Worcester, King's School 1906 54285
King's School is one of England's oldest - 14th-century or earlier. It was refounded by Henry VIII after the Dissolution. This building is College Hall, which stands on the north side of College Green and abuts the south walk of the cathedral cloisters. It has been used by King's School since 1560 but was originally the monastic refectory.

Worcester, The Cathedral Ferry 1906 54274
The ferry originated for the use of monks from the priory, to cross to their farmland on the west bank. After the Dissolution of the Monasteries the operation of the ferry passed to the Dean and Chapter of the cathedral. It lapsed in the 1950s but has since been successfully revived as a summer-only service. Edward Elgar used it regularly as a boy, crossing from his home in Worcester to his school at Lower Wick. This picture appears to show King's School pupils using it. Behind it is the Watergate, the last surviving city gate, built in 1378.

Worcester, The War Memorial 1923 73753
Erected nearly five years after the end of the Great War, this elegant memorial is built in the style of a medieval cross and stands close to the site of the original preaching cross, outside the cathedral. It is decorated with coats of arms, including that of the Worcestershire Hussars.

Worcester, The South African War Memorial 1907 59080a
This memorial stands outside the cathedral, close to the entrance to College Yard. It can not have been long built when photographed, for it commemorates those who died in the Boer War of 1899-1902. The iron railings shown in the photograph are no longer there, having been salvaged for scrap in World War Two.

Worcester, College Yard 1925 76792

The shop displaying local views (postcards) and Royal Worcester china (the obvious souvenir) is perfectly placed to catch tourists flocking to the cathedral, the main entrance of which is in College Yard. The shop is still there today, now selling high quality antiques (including Royal Worcester) to the wealthier tourists.

Worcester, College Yard 1925 76793

Note the raised pavement outside the splendid Georgian houses leading to the cathedral. The charnel house used to stand here and centuries of burials caused the ground to rise by 4 feet so that one had to descend steps to enter the cathedral. In the 19th century the road was dug out but higher ground remains in front of the houses.

▼ **Worcester, Edgar Tower 1910** 62627a

This fortified gateway, completed in 1369, guarded the entrance to the monastic precincts and was formerly known as St Mary's Gate or Priory Gate. It acquired the name of Edgar Tower in the 18th century because an ancient statue of 10th-century King Edgar stood above the gate. The tower was restored 1900-1912 and a new Edgar placed in the niche.

▼ **Worcester, College Green c1950** W141014

Entered through Edgar Tower (just visible here above the rooftops), or through the Watergate, College Green is a delightful quadrangle of mostly 17th- and 18th-century houses, forming part of King's School and occupying the site of Worcester Castle. It is the nearest Worcester has to a cathedral close.

▲ **Worcester, The River Severn from the Cathedral Tower c1960** W141077

We are looking upstream, towards the Abberley Hills in the distance, with the tower and spire of the otherwise demolished St Andrew's Church prominent on the right. In the foreground is the Old Palace which was, until 1842, one of the Bishop's residences. The railway bridge in the middle distance was built in 1860 (though the girder section dates only from 1904), part of a notable 1½-mile viaduct and embankment taking the Worcester-Hereford line across the city from Henwick to Shrub Hill. It has 68 arches, including the first brick arch to be built on the skew.

◀ **Worcester, The Malvern Hills from the Cathedral Tower c1960** W141080
Thankfully, this view is not greatly changed today, though Great Malvern has crept further across the hills and the suburbs in the middle distance have expanded. At the extreme centre left you can see Diglis, with its locks, docks and weir. This is where the Worcester and Birmingham Canal was joined to the River Severn in 1815.

Worcester, Ye Old Deanery, Lich Street 1907 59081
Lich Street linked High Street to Friar Street and Sidbury. It was crammed with medieval buildings and spanned by
the cathedral lych (or lich) gate, but had fallen into decline by the early years of the 20th century. Sadly, but
predictably, restoration was not considered and it was completely swept away in the 1960s.

Worcester, Lych Gate 1906 54284
The Lych Gate gave access to the cathedral burial ground. By 1965 it was the last surviving cathedral lych gate in Britain, but was demolished, along with Lich Street, to create a dire shopping precinct. The posters on the wall advertise Midland Railway excursions to Blackpool and Weston-super-Mare, promising some hard-earned fun for Worcester's wage slaves.

Worcester, St Andrew's Spire c1960 W141092
St Andrew's Church was demolished in 1947 but the medieval tower, with its elegant spire of 1751, was allowed to remain. It is known to Worcester folk as the Glover's Needle because of its slenderness and height, and because this part of town was the main gloving area when the trade still flourished. In 1801, while repairs to the spire were in progress, a barber shaved customers on top of it and a china painter decorated a cup. On another occasion a wine merchant shared a bottle of port up there with the editor of the 'Worcester Chronicle'.

Worcester, The Guildhall 1899   44011
Situated near the south end of High Street, this is generally regarded as the finest civic building of its period in the country. The design of a local man, Thomas White, it was built 1721-23, replacing the original timber-framed Guildhall. The city's principal civic building, it houses the Assembly Room and Mayor's Parlour. The niched effigies on the facade are of Charles I, Charles II and Queen Anne. An enjoyable detail, not fully visible in this picture, is the demon's head nailed by its ears above the door, traditionally claimed to represent Oliver Cromwell.

Worcester, The Guildhall 1936 87351
Incredibly, the Guildhall only narrowly escaped demolition in the 1870s, when Alfred Waterhouse (architect of Manchester Town Hall) presented a plan for its replacement. Waterhouse's rival, Sir George Gilbert Scott, wrote to the town clerk in protest and his letter was published in the magazine 'The Builder'. He suggested the Guildhall's demolition would gain Worcester "a most unenviable notoriety". His letter helped to save it and in 1878 a decision was made to restore the building to a plan proposed by Scott and city architect Henry Rowe. Later, in the 1960s, Worcester's redevelopment did earn it the notoriety foreseen by Scott.

▼ Worcester, High Street c1950 W141015

Looking north along High Street, the prominent clock on the right catches the eye. It was given in 1849 by Mayor Richard Padmore and projects into the street over a site once occupied by the King's Head Inn, first mentioned in 1717. The inn had a theatre in its yard but in 1779 a proper theatre opened in Angel Street and from then on the King's Head hosted a market instead. In 1804 the inn was demolished and replaced by a purpose-built market hall. This was itself demolished in the 1960s.

▼ Worcester, High Street c1950 W141020

The crowds present in this view suggest a Saturday morning. This is the north end of High Street, which seems to have had an abundance of shoe shops in 1950: Trueform (on the left) was a popular chain for decades, and Olivers (on the right), is still trading today - but who now remembers Dick's Central Boot Stores?

▲ Worcester, High Street c1950 W141026

Perhaps the most striking thing about this picture, to modern eyes, is the long line of cars, for High Street is now pedestrianised. The cars have been replaced with trees (complete with a huge wagtail roost in winter). The Shakespeare Café, on the right, is presumably hoping to pull in tourists by appropriating the Warwickshire bard.

Worcester, The Cross 1896 38931
What an evocative picture this is, taken in the days before motorised transport. Horse-drawn trams began in Worcester in 1881 with three routes, all of them passing through The Cross. The trams were single-deck and one horse-power until 1893, when updating brought double-decker cars pulled by two horses. Worcester Tramways boosted its income by turning the trams into mobile advertising hoardings for city companies such as Lewis Clarke & Co, a brewery based in Angel Place 1895-1970. The city's trams were horse-powered until 1904 when electrification put them out to grass.

**Worcester
High Street 1931**

84570

Summer sunshine has brought out the flowery frocks, but the ladies will still not venture out without their hats. A passenger boards a Midland Red bus in the centre, perhaps off for a day's walking in the Malvern Hills. Some familiar names here include Lawley's china shop and the shoe-seller Stead & Simpson, both long-established chains still trading today.

▼ **Worcester, The Cross 1899** 44010
The Star Tea Company boldly displays its wares, without the awnings employed by many of the other traders in this superb scene. Just look at the wonderful streetscape on the west side. Buildings of different heights, different widths, some with dormers, some without, some mansarded, some not; but basically almost all are Georgian in style, bringing harmony to glorious variety.

▼ **Worcester, The Cross 1923** 73756
The policeman on traffic duty in this scene seems to be having an easy time of it, with nothing but bicycles to worry about, though a tram is just visible in the distance. Notice the charming old sign for the Arcade Cinema, which opened in 1912, making it the city's second cinema. Sadly, it closed as early as the 1930s.

▲ **Worcester, The Cross 1931** 84569
The trams have gone and already car traffic is burgeoning. The signpost on the right, pointing the way to Malvern, Leominster and Hereford underlines The Cross's traditional role as the geographical and commercial centre of Worcester. A medieval cross stood here for centuries and an annual fair was held each September.

◀ **Worcester, The Cross c1960** W141084
The former London, City and Midland Bank has become plain Midland Bank, but familiar names such as Hepworths and H Samuel remain unchanged from earlier years, though sporting modern faciae. Traffic lights, signs and bollards are cluttering the streetscape and the charm of the past is evaporating. The northbound bus is most probably a Midland Red on its way to Birmingham.

Worcester, The Cross 1923 73755
The policeman's spiked helmet contrasts with the flat caps worn by most of the other men in this picture. Note how all the women and children are hatted too. Outside the National Provincial Bank passengers alight from an electric tram whose days are numbered - only five years after this picture was taken the trams were withdrawn from operation.

Worcester
The Cross c1960 W141083
Already, The Cross is showing signs of congestion, but for the time being people still feel relaxed enough to linger in groups chatting - The Cross was traditionally a meeting place. Note how they have finally relinquished their hats, though the shops still hide from the sun below awnings, in contrast to the dignified, neo-classical facades of the two banks opposite.

Worcester
The Foregate 1910 62626
This view is taken from the southern end of Foregate Street, looking south along The Foregate and The Cross. On the left is the Hop Market, resplendent in red terracotta. Worcester's first hop market was established in 1731 on this site and became the largest in the country. In the 1890s it was replaced by this flamboyant structure.

Worcester
Foregate Street 1936 87350
The two buildings dominating this view of the east side of Foregate Street have both been converted to other purposes. The Gaumont Cinema is a bingo hall now, and the Post Office is a J D Wetherspoon's pub, The Postal Order. Worcester's first post office was the Shades Tavern in Mealcheapen Street, first recorded in 1685.

Worcester
The Foregate c1950 W141018
1950 it may be, but the heavily laden cart on the right could come from an earlier age. Dominating this view, however, is the beautiful St Nicholas's Church on The Cross. First founded in the 12th century, it was rebuilt in the early 1730s, probably by Humphrey Hollins, a local architect. In the 1990s it was converted into a café-bar.

Worcester, Foregate Street c1950 W141019
On the left is the Star Hotel, a former coaching inn previously known as the Star and Garter. Stagecoaches departed from here daily for all parts of the country until the railways put an end to them. Presumably, however, the Star was able to benefit from the railways too, with Foregate Street Station being just across the road. The Worcester-Hereford line opened in 1860, operated by the Oxford, Worcester and Wolverhampton Railway (fondly known as the Old Worse and Worse) until absorbed into the Great Western Railway in 1863.

Worcester, The Foregate c1960 W141091
The Foregate and Foregate Street continue the line of High Street northwards and developed as a suburb many centuries ago. Civil War destruction led to a substantial rebuilding programme, resulting in a predominantly Georgian character. A hint of that can be seen here, looking north from The Cross to the railway bridge.

Worcester, Berkeley's Hospital c1960 W141067
These lovely almshouses of 1703 feature a striking life-size statue of a scarlet-coated Robert Berkeley in a niche on the chapel. A notable horticulturalist, a friend of diarist John Evelyn and a diplomat at The Hague, Berkeley bequeathed £2,000 to build and maintain the almshouses for 12 poor men and one woman, aged over 60.

Worcester
Shire Hall and Queen Victoria's Statue 1896
38927

Carved from a 17-ton block of white marble from Carrara in Tuscany, Queen Victoria looks unamused as she grasps her orb and sceptre in front of the Shire Hall. The statue is by Sir Thomas Brock and was commissioned to mark the Queen's Golden Jubilee of 1887. It was unveiled in 1890.

Worcester
The Victoria Institute 1896   38929
Newly built at the time of this photo, the Victoria Institute combined library, museum and a school of art and science in one building. Today, the school has been replaced by an art gallery. The first city library was founded in Angel Street in 1790 and had to move premises twice before the Victoria Institute at last provided adequate facilities.

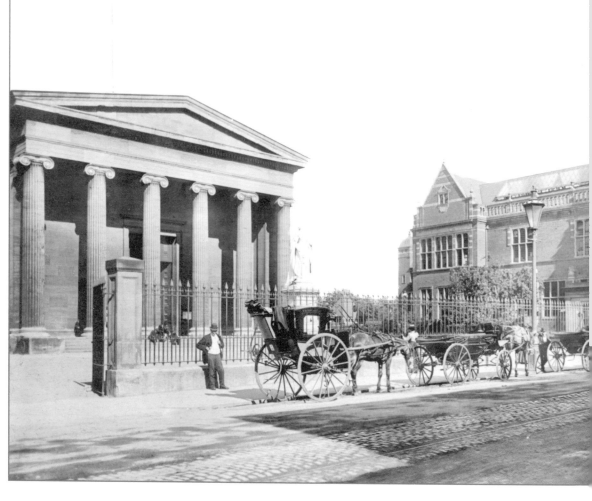

◄ **Worcester
The Tything 1936**
87347
The Tything is the
northern continuation of
Foregate Street and
ribbon development
began here centuries
ago. Yet it was
intermittent, and well
into the 19th century
there were fields on
both sides of the road,
while the postal address
was 'near Worcester'.
Part of a hamlet called
Whistones, it was
absorbed into the city
only in 1835.

◄ Worcester, Shire Hall and Victoria Institute 1899 44008

Horse-drawn cabs wait for custom outside the imposing neo-Classical Shire Hall, built 1834-5 by Charles Day of Bristol, and Henry Rowe, Worcester's own city architect. Its massive portico of fluted Ionic columns contrasts with the little gazebo-like structure which served as a rest hut for the cabbies.

▼ Worcester, The High School 1906 57108

Britannia House, on Upper Tything, was designed by Thomas White as a mansion for the Somers family. It became a boys' school in the 1860s but by the time of this photograph it had become Worcester High School for Girls. In 1914 it became (and remains) the Alice Ottley School for Girls, in honour of its first headmistress.

◄ Worcester, The Royal Grammar School 1907 59080

This is one of the oldest schools in the country. Some believe it was founded in the 7th century, but the first documentary reference was in 1291. Elizabeth I granted it a royal charter in 1561, at which time it was located in St Swithin's Street, only moving to its present location on Upper Tything in 1868.

CHURCH STREET

J & F. HALL.

**Worcester
The Shambles c1950**

W141025

The most famous Shambles is in York but many towns had their shambles or meat market at one time. This was Worcester's and until the 1930s many of the butchers' shops had their own slaughterhouses at the rear of their premises. Seedsmen, a china shop, and the popular ironmongers J and F Hall, also traded here.

▼ **Worcester, Queen Elizabeth's House 1896** 38933

Occupying the corner of The Trinity and Trinity Street, this timber-framed survivor recalls the visit of Queen Elizabeth I to Worcester in 1575. Tradition has it that she addressed the citizens from its balcony but it is more likely it was named after her because of endowments she made to Trinity Hospital, of which this building formed a part. In 1891 it was threatened with demolition when improvements were scheduled for Trinity Passage, which ran underneath it. Fortunately, cash was raised to pay for its rescue: it was jacked up and moved on greased rails a few yards to the right.

▼ **Worcester, St Swithin's Street c1950** W141024

Boots has moved to a prime site on High Street and has been replaced by a modern building occupied by a building society. St Swithun's Church can just be glimpsed (look for the pinnacle) near the centre of the picture. Built in 1736, it is claimed to be one of the most perfect churches of its period in Britain.

▲ **Worcester, Old House in the Corn Market c1890**
W141508

A carved inscription above the left-hand lower window reads 'Love God WB 1577 RD Honor Kinge'. Since the photograph was taken an inscription has been painted above the right-hand window, reading 'Ye Olde Kinge Charles House'. This has led many to believe that this is the house from which Charles II so famously escaped after the Battle of Worcester, running out of the back door as his pursuers came in at the front. However, that King Charles House is round the corner on New Street. But it does bear the same date - 1577 - so perhaps both were part of the same building.

◀ **Worcester, Silver Street c1950** W141012
Silver Street originally stood just outside the city walls, linking Lowesmoor with Corn Market, until it was cut off from the latter by the construction of City Walls Road. It was the original site of Worcester General Infirmary, which opened in 1746 with just 30 beds. In 1771 it was replaced by the present infirmary in Castle Street.

◄ **Worcester**
Friar Street c1950 W141013
Comparing this view of Friar Street to the similar one taken in 1891, shows that the three-gabled building next to the car has had a coat of render stripped away to expose its timbers, while the shop on the far left has been smartened up (losing some of its charm in the process) to house Elt's shoe shop. This is a familiar name in Worcester. Albert Edward Elt started selling shoes in 1872 and the family owns several shops today, though there is no longer one on Friar Street.

◄ Worcester, Friar Street 1891 29321

Young lads in knickerbockers, and one in a sailor suit, pose self-consciously for the camera in Friar Street. Little changed today, this is the finest street in Worcester, with its timber-framing, gables and wonderfully uneven roofline. For centuries Friar Street has been occupied by small tradesmen, such as the hardware merchant whose tin buckets are displayed so exuberantly outside the shop on the left. In the 19th century many were Nonconformists, such as Quakers, and next but one to the hardware shop can be seen the entrance, now demolished, of a Nonconformist mission hall.

▼ Worcester, Friar Street Old House 1891 29322

This shows the rear of the house now known as Greyfriars. It was built for a wealthy citizen in 1480 next to a Franciscan friary, but was later divided into tenements and soon deteriorated into a squalid slum. It was restored in the 20th century by Mr and Mrs Matley Moore who then presented it to the National Trust.

◄ Worcester, Greyfriars Friar Street c1960

W141082

Another view of Greyfriars, this time showing the impressive front elevation. The friary from which it took its name was founded by the Franciscan order in 1235. The Franciscans, or Grey Friars, were a mendicant order founded by St Francis of Assisi. Their friary in Worcester was of considerable importance, exercising authority over others in the West Midlands.

Worcester
Broad Street c1955
W141022
As you can see from this
picture, Broad Street is
anything but. Fortunately,
it has now been
pedestrianised. It has
been an important
commercial street for
centuries and during late
medieval times was the
location for a sheep
market. It was in Broad
Street in 1837 that a
certain Mr Lea and Mr
Perrins first started selling
their famous sauce.

Worcester, Laslett's Almshouses 1910 62625a

The almshouses stand at the junction of Friar Street and Union Street on a site previously occupied by the city gaol. In 1869 the gaol was sold to William Laslett, a solicitor, Liberal MP and benefactor, who adapted it to accommodate elderly married couples of limited means. In 1910 the gaol was demolished and replaced with this mock-Tudor building.

Worcester, Broad Street c1950 W141016

When the new Worcester Bridge opened in 1781 it gave Broad Street quite a boost, helping it to support three coaching inns. The Unicorn Inn and the Bell Hotel were demolished long ago but the splendid Crown Hotel is still trading, though its former yard has been converted into a shopping arcade, Crown Passage.

Worcester
Angel Place c1950 W141037
Judging by the lack of umbrellas, the rain falling on Angel Place must have
taken Worcester by surprise. Fortunately, those waiting for a bus home
can take cover under shelter (on the left). For many years Angel Place
served as one of the city's two desperately inadequate bus terminals, but
now accommodates Crowngate Market.

The Westside and Beyond

Worcester
The Bridge 1936 87346
Note the Malvern Hills in the distance, and the tower of St John's
Church, adding interest to this view of Worcester Bridge, which
had been substantially widened just a few years before the picture
was taken. Over on the Westside you can see Cripplegate Park,
created in 1930 on the site of the long-established
Wilesmith's timber yard.

Worcester, New Road 1906 54277a

An early traveller from Worcester bound for the Westside would first cross the bridge, then follow a causeway across flood meadows before trudging up narrow, winding Cripplegate to St John's. Only in 1781 did the construction, a little way downstream, of Worcester Bridge and New Road provide a direct route.

Worcester, Surrey v Worcester Cricket Match 1907 59082a

Overlooked by the cathedral, New Road is one of the most attractive grounds in the country. There has been a county side since 1847 but the present club dates from 1865. First class county status was achieved in 1899, even though the county ground was simply three hay fields, rented from the Dean and Chapter of the cathedral.

Worcester, St John's 1925 76851
Today the tramlines have gone, and the traffic is dreadful. Other than that, the ancient heart of St John's still looks very like this picture, its Georgian and Victorian facades mostly unspoilt - on the upper floors at least. Sadly, the charming enamel signs on the left, advertising Rowntree's and Cadbury's chocolate, have long since gone.

◄**Worcester, St John's Church 1904** 51853
St John in Bedwardine, to give it its full name, is a 12th-century church of considerable interest, despite Victorian alterations. It was founded as a chapel for farm workers, replacing St Cuthbert's at nearby Lower Wick. The Parliamentarians used it in the Civil War and grooves on the window ledges are said to have been made by soldiers sharpening weapons.

◄ **Worcester, St John's 1925** 76850
In medieval times St John's was a cluster of timber-framed houses round the church, and a busy junction on the roads to Malvern, Hereford and Leominster. It was absorbed into the city in 1837 and has expanded considerably since. It was in St John's that the Worcester Pearmain was discovered in 1872 in the market garden of William Hales.

▼ **Broadwas, Butts Bank Farm c1955** B425002
Broadwas is a pleasant village in pastoral Teme Valley farmland, six miles west of Worcester. This handsome farmhouse survives unaltered and unspoilt today, though no longer part of a working farm. It stands on a quiet lane on Weston Hill, north-east of Broadwas, with magnificent views across the valley to the Malverns.

◄ **Broadwas The River Teme c1955**
B425004
The pollarded willows by the river are typical of the lower Teme Valley. Fortunately, willows are well able to withstand the annual floods. In the distance is a glimpse of the timber bell turret of St Mary Magdalene's Church at Broadwas. The church stands close to the river by Broadwas Court and dates mostly from c1200.

North of the City

Worcester
The Racecourse c1965 W141105
The Racecourse occupies part of Pitchcroft, which is where the
Romans dumped the slag from their iron workings. The slag was
removed in the 17th century but Pitchcroft remained undeveloped,
acting as a venue for fairs, circuses, military camps and musters.
Horse racing first took place in 1718 and the Grandstand
was built in 1823.

Worcester, The River Severn and Grandstand 1906 57109
The photographer is standing on the west bank looking across to the original 1823 grandstand on the edge of Pitchcroft. The grandstand included an hotel and was operated by a local charity, St Oswald's Hospital, until the City bought it in 1897, two years after buying Pitchcroft itself. The grandstand was demolished in 1974 and its replacement opened in 1976.

Worcester, The Regatta 1910 62325
Wearing long elegant dresses and impractically large hats, these Edwardian women are gathered with their menfolk on Pitchcroft to enjoy the ever-fascinating sight of other people messing about in boats. The grandstand is visible at top left, surrounded by a large crowd, while more crowds throng the Westside below Hylton Road.

Worcester, The Regatta 1910 62327

Taken from the Westside, this picture reveals that a fair is taking place on Pitchcroft to accompany the Regatta. It was in 1910, possibly on this same occasion, that a Bleriot aeroplane took off from Pitchcroft - the first powered plane seen in the city. Sadly, poor crowd control led to the death of a woman who got too close to the propeller. In 1911, a balloon took off from Pitchcroft during celebrations for the coronation of George V, and even today people taking scenic flights with Worcester Balloons still start their journey on Pitchcroft.

Worcester, The Dog and Duck Ferry 1923 73762

Near the northern end of Pitchcroft, a ferry crossed the Severn to a watermen's inn and a small quay, originally built to serve villages to the west, such as Martley. Donkeys carried the goods up the steep slope from the wharf and the path up is still known as Ferry Bank. The Dog and Duck probably derived its name from a pursuit engaged in by watermen, in which dogs were set on ducks rendered flightless by wing clipping. Most of these buildings still stand, but are altered almost out of recognition.

Worcester
The Old Water Tower
from the River Severn 1906 54275

The old water tower forms an interesting backdrop to a pleasure steamer heading upstream. From the 1880s to the 1930s, taking a steamer trip from Worcester was an enormously popular pastime. Boats travelled upriver to Stourport (the northern limit of navigation) or downriver as far as Tewkesbury.

Worcester
The Old Water Tower 1906 54276

Situated at Barbourne, the tower originally formed a vital component of the waterworks, built in 1770. A waterwheel lifted water from the Severn to a storage tank at the top of the tower. It became redundant when a new waterworks was built and it was converted into dwellings before eventually being demolished in the 1960s.

**Worcester
The Kepax Ferry
1906** 54272
A crowded steamer
passes Kepax Ferry on
the northern edge of
town, close to the old
waterworks. There were
six houses at Kepax and
around 1906 all were
occupied by the Bailey
family. The Ferryman,
Mr Bailey, had the Ferry
House and his married
daughters had the
others. Unsurprisingly,
Kepax Ferry was known
as Bailey's Boat.

◄ Worcester, Gheluvelt Park c1965
W141112

It may look typical, but the park has an unusual distinction in that it forms Worcester's memorial to the Great War. It was acquired by the council in the 1920s and named after the Flemish village where the Worcestershire Regiment made a heroic charge in October 1914, helping to save Ypres and halting the German advance on the channel ports. But for 'the gallant Worcesters' the war might otherwise have been lost at this early stage. The building in the park of these homes for disabled veterans added a valuable practical touch to the memorial.

◄ Worcester Gheluvelt Park 1936

87353

This photo shows the stereotypical municipal park with its formal gardens, water features and children's playground. There are also sports facilities and a bandstand. It was created on the site of an 18th-century house with 18 acres of private parkland by Barbourne Brook.

▼ Worcester, Bevere Lock and Weir 1891 29293b

Bevere Island is the second largest of all the natural islets in the River Severn and used to be a refuge for the citizens. It was here they came to escape Danish raiders in 1041, and here too they tried to flee the plague in 1637. As a result, the island was often referred to as The Camp. An iron footbridge connects Bevere Island to the east bank and a lock, built in 1844, to the west bank. The name comes from Beaver Island but the beavers died out over 1,000 years ago.

◄ Hallow, The Post Office and Oakleigh Avenue c1955 H152001

Hallow has changed a great deal since it was visited by Queen Elizabeth I in 1575, and quite a lot since 1955, when this picture was taken. But the Post Office still occupies this same house, even if it is much modernised and extended. Sadly, the little circle of grass has long since fallen victim to the demands of modern traffic.

Hallow, The Village c1955 H152005
The charming old signpost indicating Shoulton, Peachley and Broadheath, has gone. So have the patch of grass, the thatched cottage and the trees. The Royal Oak is still there, though it looks very different now. The pub's name refers to the Shropshire tree in which Charles II hid from his pursuers after the Battle of Worcester in 1651.

Hallow, The Village c1955 H152006
The old brick barn still stands, but these lovely cottages have been replaced by two red-brick modern houses. In the distance you can see the Green and beyond it the tall spire of the church of St Philip and St James, built in 1869 with sandstone from nearby Holt. The tower and spire were added later.

Hallow, The Green c1955 H152007

This attractive view is little changed today, except that the Green, predictably, is kept close-mown now, and woe betide any daisy that shows its head. The spindly oak tree is now a splendid specimen and several more trees have been planted. Just behind the car is Church Lane, which leads to Hallow Old Churchyard. While nothing remains of the medieval church, the leafy old graveyard has become something of a wildlife refuge. An adjacent footpath leads to a viewpoint over the Severn Valley and then down past Hallow Park, where Elizabeth I hunted in 1575, to the river itself.

Holt Fleet, Holt Fleet Bridge 1896 38934

There was a ferry at Holt Fleet long before Thomas Telford's graceful bridge was opened in 1828. For many years an adjacent inn had catered for ferry passengers and in 1844, after improvements to the navigation, which included the construction of a lock and weir upstream from the bridge, the inn became an important pleasure resort for steamer passengers.

**Ombersley
The Post Office 1910**

62630

Posing for the photographer, or genuinely posting a letter? It is hard to tell, but the beribboned young girl with the ringlets and the delightfully impractical dress is worth a picture. In the background, beyond the chestnut trees, is St Andrew's Church, built 1825-29 in the Decorated style to the design of Thomas Rickman.

Ombersley, The Village 1897 38935
Predominantly 'black and white', this Severnside village is a gem of a place, with more than 40 Grade II Listed Buildings. The King's Arms, on the right in this picture, is one of them. It dates from c1450 and Charles II is said to have spent a night there after the Battle of Worcester in 1651.

Ombersley, The Village c1955 018008
This view of Ombersley's main street gives an idea of the range of facilities in the village. A shop, a café, a guest house and two pubs feature in this view, and all are still there today in one form or another. Note the CTC sign outside the café/B&B, extending a welcome to members of the Cyclists' Touring Club.

Ombersley, The Village Cross 1910 62628
This churchyard cross dates from the 15th century, so it is about 400 years older than the present church.
However, St Andrew's was built to replace a 13th-century church, only part of which still stands and now serves as
a mausoleum for the Sandys family of Ombersley Court.

South of the City

Worcester, Battenhall Road 1907 59078
Battenhall lies off London Road and was first
recorded in Norman times, when the Poer family
held the manor for the annual rent of one lamprey.
It later belonged to the priors of Worcester, who
made a deer park and built a palace. After the
Dissolution, part of the estate went to Worcester
Cathedral and the rest fell into the hands of a
succession of different families. The modern suburb
originated with a Royal Agricultural Society show
held at Battenhall in 1863. To create suitable access
to the show, Battenhall Road was made and a
residential suburb inevitably followed.

▼ **Worcester, Battenhall Road 1907** 59079
Mary Tudor stayed at Battenhall as a child, when her father Henry VIII banished her
from Court. When she became Queen she made Sir John Bourne of Battenhall her
Secretary of State. Some years later, Sir Thomas Bromley of Battenhall was Lord
Chancellor to Elizabeth I, who stayed at Battenhall on her 1575 visit to Worcester.

▼ **Worcester, Battenhall Lodge 1907** 59077
In view of all Battenhall's Tudor connections it seems fitting that
Battenhall Lodge should be Tudor in style, though built by Victorians.
It was the gatehouse to Battenhall Mount, which was built as a private
house but later served as a convalescent hospital for wounded soldiers
before it became St Mary's Convent.

▲ **Worcester
St Dunstan's Crescen
1907** 59076
This Battenhall street is
typical of late
Victorian/Edwardian
housing intended for th
'lower middle classes'.
Though the
overwhelming impressi
is one of a solid, well-
proportioned lack of
pretension, a closer loo
also reveals attractive
detailing such as the
balustraded balconies
above the bay windows
on the left and the
ornamental ironwork,
most obvious bottom le

Worcester, The Junction of the Rivers Teme and Severn 1906 54278
The River Teme rises in the Kerry Hills of Radnorshire and flows through 75 miles of beautiful countryside before it meets the River Severn just south of Worcester. The Battle of Powick Bridge took place nearby in 1642 and, more importantly, much of the action of the Battle of Worcester in 1651 took place on and around this site.

Powick
The Roundabout
c1955 P108002
Powick is best known
for the Battle of Powick
Bridge, the first
skirmish of the Civil War
in 1642. It lasted only
15 minutes or so but it
left over 50
Parliamentary troopers
dead, some of them
drowned in the Teme.
All the Royalist officers
were injured too, except
for their commander,
the dashing
Prince Rupert.

Powick
The Village c1955 P108502
Apart from the battle, Powick's other main claim to fame is Powick
Mills next to the bridge where the battle took place. Domesday
Book (1086) recorded two mills here but it was in 1893 that
Worcester Corporation purchased the site and built a combined
steam- and water-driven hydroelectric facility (the first of its kind).
It provided half the city's supply until Worcester Power Station
became operational in the early 20th century. Powick Mills
continued to supply power until the 1950s. The mill buildings have
recently been converted into apartments.

Index

Frith Book Co Titles

www.francisfrith.co.uk

The Frith Book Company publishes over 100 new titles each year. A selection of those currently available are listed below. For latest catalogue please contact Frith Book Co.

Town Books 96pages, approx 100 photos. County and Themed Books 128pages, approx 150 photos (unless specified). All titles hardback laminated case and jacket except those indicated pb (paperback)

Amersham, Chesham & Rickmansworth (pb)	1-85937-340-2	£9.99	Dorset (pb)	1-85937-269-4	£9.99
Ancient Monuments & Stone Circles	1-85937-143-4	£17.99	Dorset Churches	1-85937-172-8	£17.99
Aylesbury (pb)	1-85937-227-9	£9.99	Dorset Coast (pb)	1-85937-299-6	£9.99
Bakewell	1-85937-113-2	£12.99	Dorset Living Memories	1-85937-210-4	£14.99
Barnstaple (pb)	1-85937-300-3	£9.99	Down the Severn	1-85937-118-3	£14.99
Bath (pb)	1-85937419-0	£9.99	Down the Thames (pb)	1-85937-278-3	£9.99
Bedford (pb)	1-85937-205-8	£9.99	Down the Trent	1-85937-311-9	£14.99
Belfast (pb)	1-85937-303-8	£9.99	Dublin (pb)	1-85937-231-7	£9.99
Berkshire (pb)	1-85937-191-4	£9.99	East Anglia (pb)	1-85937-265-1	£9.99
Berkshire Churches	1-85937-170-1	£17.99	East London	1-85937-080-2	£14.99
Blackpool (pb)	1-85937-382-8	£9.99	East Sussex	1-85937-130-2	£14.99
Bognor Regis (pb)	1-85937-431-x	£9.99	Eastbourne	1-85937-061-6	£12.99
Bournemouth	1-85937-067-5	£12.99	Edinburgh (pb)	1-85937-193-0	£8.99
Bradford (pb)	1-85937-204-x	£9.99	England in the 1880's	1-85937-331-3	£17.99
Brighton & Hove(pb)	1-85937-192-2	£8.99	English Castles (pb)	1-85937-434-4	£9.99
Bristol (pb)	1-85937-264-3	£9.99	English Country Houses	1-85937-161-2	£17.99
British Life A Century Ago (pb)	1-85937-213-9	£9.99	Essex (pb)	1-85937-270-8	£9.99
Buckinghamshire (pb)	1-85937-200-7	£9.99	Exeter	1-85937-126-4	£12.99
Camberley (pb)	1-85937-222-8	£9.99	Exmoor	1-85937-132-9	£14.99
Cambridge (pb)	1-85937-422-0	£9.99	Falmouth	1-85937-066-7	£12.99
Cambridgeshire (pb)	1-85937-420-4	£9.99	Folkestone (pb)	1-85937-124-8	£9.99
Canals & Waterways (pb)	1-85937-291-0	£9.99	Glasgow (pb)	1-85937-190-6	£9.99
Canterbury Cathedral (pb)	1-85937-179-5	£9.99	Gloucestershire	1-85937-102-7	£14.99
Cardiff (pb)	1-85937-093-4	£9.99	Great Yarmouth (pb)	1-85937-426-3	£9.99
Carmarthenshire	1-85937-216-3	£14.99	Greater Manchester (pb)	1-85937-266-x	£9.99
Chelmsford (pb)	1-85937-310-0	£9.99	Guildford (pb)	1-85937-410-7	£9.99
Cheltenham (pb)	1-85937-095-0	£9.99	Hampshire (pb)	1-85937-279-1	£9.99
Cheshire (pb)	1-85937-271-6	£9.99	Hampshire Churches (pb)	1-85937-207-4	£9.99
Chester	1-85937-090-x	£12.99	Harrogate	1-85937-423-9	£9.99
Chesterfield	1-85937-378-x	£9.99	Hastings & Bexhill (pb)	1-85937-131-0	£9.99
Chichester (pb)	1-85937-228-7	£9.99	Heart of Lancashire (pb)	1-85937-197-3	£9.99
Colchester (pb)	1-85937-188-4	£8.99	Helston (pb)	1-85937-214-7	£9.99
Cornish Coast	1-85937-163-9	£14.99	Hereford (pb)	1-85937-175-2	£9.99
Cornwall (pb)	1-85937-229-5	£9.99	Herefordshire	1-85937-174-4	£14.99
Cornwall Living Memories	1-85937-248-1	£14.99	Hertfordshire (pb)	1-85937-247-3	£9.99
Cotswolds (pb)	1-85937-230-9	£9.99	Horsham (pb)	1-85937-432-8	£9.99
Cotswolds Living Memories	1-85937-255-4	£14.99	Humberside	1-85937-215-5	£14.99
County Durham	1-85937-123-x	£14.99	Hythe, Romney Marsh & Ashford	1-85937-256-2	£9.99
Croydon Living Memories	1-85937-162-0	£9.99	Ipswich (pb)	1-85937-424-7	£9.99
Cumbria	1-85937-101-9	£14.99	Ireland (pb)	1-85937-181-7	£9.99
Dartmoor	1-85937-145-0	£14.99	Isle of Man (pb)	1-85937-268-6	£9.99
Derby (pb)	1-85937-367-4	£9.99	Isles of Scilly	1-85937-136-1	£14.99
Derbyshire (pb)	1-85937-196-5	£9.99	Isle of Wight (pb)	1-85937-429-8	£9.99
Devon (pb)	1-85937-297-x	£9.99	Isle of Wight Living Memories	1-85937-304-6	£14.99

Available from your local bookshop or from the publisher

Frith Book Co Titles (continued)

Kent (pb)	1-85937-189-2	£9.99
Kent Living Memories	1-85937-125-6	£14.99
Lake District (pb)	1-85937-275-9	£9.99
Lancaster, Morecambe & Heysham (pb)	1-85937-233-3	£9.99
Leeds (pb)	1-85937-202-3	£9.99
Leicester	1-85937-073-x	£12.99
Leicestershire (pb)	1-85937-185-x	£9.99
Lighthouses	1-85937-257-0	£17.99
Lincolnshire (pb)	1-85937-433-6	£9.99
Liverpool & Merseyside (pb)	1-85937-234-1	£9.99
London (pb)	1-85937-183-3	£9.99
Ludlow (pb)	1-85937-176-0	£9.99
Luton (pb)	1-85937-235-x	£9.99
Maidstone	1-85937-056-x	£14.99
Manchester (pb)	1-85937-198-1	£9.99
Middlesex	1-85937-158-2	£14.99
New Forest	1-85937-128-0	£14.99
Newark (pb)	1-85937-366-6	£9.99
Newport, Wales (pb)	1-85937-258-9	£9.99
Newquay (pb)	1-85937-421-2	£9.99
Norfolk (pb)	1-85937-195-7	£9.99
Norfolk Living Memories	1-85937-217-1	£14.99
Northamptonshire	1-85937-150-7	£14.99
Northumberland Tyne & Wear (pb)	1-85937-281-3	£9.99
North Devon Coast	1-85937-146-9	£14.99
North Devon Living Memories	1-85937-261-9	£14.99
North London	1-85937-206-6	£14.99
North Wales (pb)	1-85937-298-8	£9.99
North Yorkshire (pb)	1-85937-236-8	£9.99
Norwich (pb)	1-85937-194-9	£8.99
Nottingham (pb)	1-85937-324-0	£9.99
Nottinghamshire (pb)	1-85937-187-6	£9.99
Oxford (pb)	1-85937-411-5	£9.99
Oxfordshire (pb)	1-85937-430-1	£9.99
Peak District (pb)	1-85937-280-5	£9.99
Penzance	1-85937-069-1	£12.99
Peterborough (pb)	1-85937-219-8	£9.99
Piers	1-85937-237-6	£17.99
Plymouth	1-85937-119-1	£12.99
Poole & Sandbanks (pb)	1-85937-251-1	£9.99
Preston (pb)	1-85937-212-0	£9.99
Reading (pb)	1-85937-238-4	£9.99
Romford (pb)	1-85937-319-4	£9.99
Salisbury (pb)	1-85937-239-2	£9.99
Scarborough (pb)	1-85937-379-8	£9.99
St ALbans (pb)	1-85937-341-0	£9.99
St Ives (pb)	1-85937415-8	£9.99
Scotland (pb)	1-85937-182-5	£9.99
Scottish Castles (pb)	1-85937-323-2	£9.99
Sevenoaks & Tunbridge	1-85937-057-8	£12.99
Sheffield, South Yorks (pb)	1-85937-267-8	£9.99
Shrewsbury (pb)	1-85937-325-9	£9.99
Shropshire (pb)	1-85937-326-7	£9.99
Somerset	1-85937-153-1	£14.99
South Devon Coast	1-85937-107-8	£14.99
South Devon Living Memories	1-85937-168-x	£14.99
South Hams	1-85937-220-1	£14.99
Southampton (pb)	1-85937-427-1	£9.99
Southport (pb)	1-85937-425-5	£9.99
Staffordshire	1-85937-047-0	£12.99
Stratford upon Avon	1-85937-098-5	£12.99
Suffolk (pb)	1-85937-221-x	£9.99
Suffolk Coast	1-85937-259-7	£14.99
Surrey (pb)	1-85937-240-6	£9.99
Sussex (pb)	1-85937-184-1	£9.99
Swansea (pb)	1-85937-167-1	£9.99
Tees Valley & Cleveland	1-85937-211-2	£14.99
Thanet (pb)	1-85937-116-7	£9.99
Tiverton (pb)	1-85937-178-7	£9.99
Torbay	1-85937-063-2	£12.99
Truro	1-85937-147-7	£12.99
Victorian and Edwardian Cornwall	1-85937-252-x	£14.99
Victorian & Edwardian Devon	1-85937-253-8	£14.99
Victorian & Edwardian Kent	1-85937-149-3	£14.99
Vic & Ed Maritime Album	1-85937-144-2	£17.99
Victorian and Edwardian Sussex	1-85937-157-4	£14.99
Victorian & Edwardian Yorkshire	1-85937-154-x	£14.99
Victorian Seaside	1-85937-159-0	£17.99
Villages of Devon (pb)	1-85937-293-7	£9.99
Villages of Kent (pb)	1-85937-294-5	£9.99
Villages of Sussex (pb)	1-85937-295-3	£9.99
Warwickshire (pb)	1-85937-203-1	£9.99
Welsh Castles (pb)	1-85937-322-4	£9.99
West Midlands (pb)	1-85937-289-9	£9.99
West Sussex	1-85937-148-5	£14.99
West Yorkshire (pb)	1-85937-201-5	£9.99
Weymouth (pb)	1-85937-209-0	£9.99
Wiltshire (pb)	1-85937-277-5	£9.99
Wiltshire Churches (pb)	1-85937-171-x	£9.99
Wiltshire Living Memories	1-85937-245-7	£14.99
Winchester (pb)	1-85937-428-x	£9.99
Windmills & Watermills	1-85937-242-2	£17.99
Worcester (pb)	1-85937-165-5	£9.99
Worcestershire	1-85937-152-3	£14.99
York (pb)	1-85937-199-x	£9.99
Yorkshire (pb)	1-85937-186-8	£9.99
Yorkshire Living Memories	1-85937-166-3	£14.99

See Frith books on the internet www.francisfrith.co.uk

FRITH PRODUCTS & SERVICES

Francis Frith would doubtless be pleased to know that the pioneering publishing venture he started in 1860 still continues today. A hundred and forty years later, The Francis Frith Collection continues in the same innovative tradition and is now one of the foremost publishers of vintage photographs in the world. Some of the current activities include:

Interior Decoration

Today Frith's photographs can be seen framed and as giant wall murals in thousands of pubs, restaurants, hotels, banks, retail stores and other public buildings throughout the country. In every case they enhance the unique local atmosphere of the places they depict and provide reminders of gentler days in an increasingly busy and frenetic world.

Product Promotions

Frith products are used by many major companies to promote the sales of their own products or to reinforce their own history and heritage. Frith promotions have been used by Hovis bread, Courage beers, Scots Porage Oats, Colman's mustard, Cadbury's foods, Mellow Birds coffee, Dunhill pipe tobacco, Guinness, and Bulmer's Cider.

Genealogy and Family History

As the interest in family history and roots grows world-wide, more and more people are turning to Frith's photographs of Great Britain for images of the towns, villages and streets where their ancestors lived; and, of course, photographs of the churches and chapels where their ancestors were christened, married and buried are an essential part of every genealogy tree and family album.

Frith Products

All Frith photographs are available Framed or just as Mounted Prints and Posters (size 23 x 16 inches). These may be ordered from the address below. From time to time other products - Address Books, Calendars, Table Mats, etc - are available.

The Internet

Already twenty thousand Frith photographs can be viewed and purchased on the internet through the Frith websites and a myriad of partner sites.

For more detailed information on Frith companies and products, look at these sites:

www.francisfrith.co.uk
www.francisfrith.com
(for North American visitors)

See the complete list of Frith Books at:

www.francisfrith.co.uk

This web site is regularly updated with the latest list of publications from the Frith Book Company. If you wish to buy books relating to another part of the country that your local bookshop does not stock, you may purchase on-line.

For further information, trade, or author enquiries please contact us at the address below:
The Francis Frith Collection, Frith's Barn, Teffont, Salisbury, Wiltshire, England SP3 5QP.
Tel: +44 (0)1722 716 376 Fax: +44 (0)1722 716 881 Email: sales@francisfrith.co.uk

See Frith books on the internet www.francisfrith.co.uk

TO RECEIVE YOUR FREE MOUNTED PRINT

Mounted Print
Overall size 14 x 11 inches

Cut out this Voucher and return it with your remittance for £1.95 to cover postage and handling, to UK addresses. For overseas addresses please include £4.00 post and handling. Choose any photograph included in this book. Your SEPIA print will be A4 in size, and mounted in a cream mount with burgundy rule line, overall size 14 x 11 inches.

Order additional Mounted Prints at HALF PRICE (only £7.49 each*)

If there are further pictures you would like to order, possibly as gifts for friends and family, purchase them at half price (no additional postage and handling required).

Have your Mounted Prints framed*

For an additional £14.95 per print you can have your chosen Mounted Print framed in an elegant polished wood and gilt moulding, overall size 16 x 13 inches (no additional postage and handling required).

---

* IMPORTANT!
These special prices are only available if ordered using the original voucher on this page (no copies permitted) and at the same time as your free Mounted Print, for delivery to the same address

---

Frith Collectors' Guild

From time to time we publish a magazine of news and stories about Frith photographs and further special offers of Frith products. If you would like 12 months FREE membership, please return this form.

Send completed forms to:

The Francis Frith Collection, Frith's Barn, Teffont, Salisbury, Wiltshire SP3 5QP

Voucher for FREE and Reduced Price Frith Prints

Picture no.	Page number	Qty	Mounted @ £7.49	Framed + £14.95	Total Cost
		1	**Free of charge***	£	£
			£7.49	£	£
			£7.49	£	£
			£7.49	£	£
			£7.49	£	£
			£7.49	£	£

Please allow 28 days for delivery		*** Post & handling**	**£1.95**
Book Title		**Total Order Cost**	**£**

Please do not photocopy this voucher. Only the original is valid, so please cut it out and return it to us.

I enclose a cheque / postal order for £ . . . .
made payable to 'The Francis Frith Collection'
OR please debit my Mastercard / Visa / Switch / Amex card
(credit cards please on all overseas orders)

Number . . . .

Issue No (Switch only) . . . . .Valid from (Amex/Switch) . . . .

Expires . . . . Signature . . . .

Name Mr/Mrs/Ms . . . .

Address . . . .

. . . .

. . . .

. . . . Postcode . . . .

Daytime Tel No . . . .   Valid to 31/12/02

The Francis Frith Collectors' Guild

Please enrol me as a member for 12 months free of charge.

Name Mr/Mrs/Ms . . . .

Address . . . .

. . . .

. . . .

. . . . Postcode . . . .

Would you like to find out more about Francis Frith?

We have recently recruited some entertaining speakers who are happy to visit local groups, clubs and societies to give an illustrated talk documenting Frith's travels and photographs. If you are a member of such a group and are interested in hosting a
presentation, we would love to hear from you.

Our speakers bring with them a small selection of our local town and county books, together with sample prints. They are happy to take orders. A small proportion of the order value is donated to the group who have hosted the presentation. The talks are therefore an excellent way of fundraising for small groups and societies.

Can you help us with information about any of the Frith photographs in this book?

We are gradually compiling an historical record for each of the photographs in the Frith archive. It is always fascinating to find out the names of the people shown in the pictures, as well as insights into the shops, buildings and other features depicted.

If you recognize anyone in the photographs in this book, or if you have information not already included in the author's caption, do let us know. We would love to hear from you, and will try to publish it in future books or articles.

Our production team

Frith books are produced by a small dedicated team at offices in the converted Grade II listed 18th-century barn at Teffont near Salisbury, illustrated above. Most have worked with the Frith Collection for many years. All have in common one quality: they have a passion for the Frith Collection. The team is constantly expanding, but currently includes:

Jason Buck, John Buck, Douglas Burns, Heather Crisp, Isobel Hall, Rob Hames, Hazel Heaton, Peter Horne, James Kinnear, Tina Leary, Eliza Sackett, Terence Sackett, Sandra Sanger, Shelley Tolcher, Susanna Walker, Clive Wathen and Jenny Wathen.

Free Print – see overleaf

Six of the many fine period photographs from the world-famous Francis Frith Collection depicted in this lavishly illustrated book. Rich in detail, they offer a fascinating portrait of Worcester in years gone by.

A range of illustrated County, Town and Theme books - each illustrated with photographs from the world-famous Francis Frith Collection

FRITH
Book Co

Teffont, Salisbury SP3 5QP

www.francisfrith.co.uk

ISBN 1-85937-165-5

9 781859 371657

£9.99   Including Voucher for